Conférence Saint-Yves Luxembourg (ed.)

Rosario Livatino

An Inspirational Lawyer
Fighting Money Laundering

ROSARIO LIVATINO

AN INSPIRATIONAL LAWYER
FIGHTING MONEY LAUNDERING

CONFÉRENCE SAINT-YVES
LUXEMBOURG (ED.)

**Bibliographische Informationen der
Deutschen Nationalbibliothek**
Die Deutsche Nationalbibliothek verzeichnet
diese Publikation in der Deutschen Nationalbiblio-
graphie; detaillierte bibliographische Daten sind im
Internet über http://dnb.dnb.de abrufbar.

        www.csy.lu
        csy@cathol.lu

        Cover: Rosario Livatino
                  Drawing by William L. Simpson
        Layout: Gilberte Bodson

ISBN 978-3-7568-8536-7

Printing and publishing:
BoD – Books on Demand, Norderstedt

Table of Contents

Welcoming Words

by William Lindsay SIMPSON
President of the Catholic Law Society
of Luxembourg

This online event was organised on May 19, 2022 by several Belgian, French and Luxembourgish Catholic Law Societies.[1] The conference brought together different speakers including an EU prosecutor (Claude Eischen, European Delegated Prosecutor), a national judge (Domenico Airoma, Chief Prosecutor of Avellino), and a university professor (Filippo Vari, Università degli Studi Europea of Rome).

The purpose of the conference and of this report is to help lawyers to make sense of their legal profession by identifying "inspirational legal figures" – including blessed Rosario Livatino.

---

[1] Including: Association Belge des Juristes Catholiques, Association des Juristes Catholiques Angevins, Association des Juristes Catholiques d'Aquitaine, Cercle Affectio Societatis (Paris), Conférence Saint-Yves (Luxembourg).

Since his beatification by Pope Francis in 2021, Blessed Rosario can be considered as the new patron saint of AML lawyers and practitioners. His "inspirational life" can help us to take a step-back from our daily legal practice and think about the mission and the duties of any "Catholic Lawyer" within his own legal community.

This paper is also the opportunity to recall the absolute necessity of fighting money laundering and financing terrorism with an attempt to identify recent inspirational AML lawyers.

Introduction

by Vianney DE BAGNEAUX
President of the Catholic Law Society
of Angers (France)

Why did we choose to talk about blessed Rosario Livatino on the day of the feast of saint Yves, patron saint of judges and lawyers?

Blessed Rosario Livatino, alike saint Yves, fulfilled his vocation as a judge and as a Christian. Rosario Livatino could have easily secured a comfortable life as a member of the Italian judiciary, which would have included respectability, social recognition and individual fulfilment.

Blessed Rosario did not take this easy path and he did not resign himself to accept the *status quo*. On the contrary, he considered that his position obliged him "to serve" – and moreover – "to serve justice". Like the "faithful and wise steward whom his master made a ruler over his household", blessed Rosario considered that his duty as a judge was to act as a faithful and wise steward of the kingdom of God.

He aimed to achieve his mission in his local jurisdiction and to work not for his personal edification but as a good and faithful servant of God.

The judicial duties of blessed Rosario involved many challenges including facing endemic corruption, illegal arrangements between the local authorities, and the reign of dirty money and crime. He did not walk away and washed his hands like *Pontius Pilate* saying this is not his business. Quite the opposite: he fully embraced the difficult situation he had to face supported by his only ally, his Faith in God. He exercised his judiciary function "under the tutelage of God" as he used to write in his notebook. Blessed Rosario was murdered on September 21, 1999 by the mafia. His martyrdom made him a "martyr of justice and indirectly of Faith" according to Saint John Paul II.

The example of Blessed Rosario Livatino's life is a challenge for all of us, lawyers, judges, notaries, compliance officers, legal clerks, or any woman or man practicing law. Are we aware of the duties that God has entrusted to us in the realm of justice and law? Are we acting with the same faith and courage as shown by blessed Rosario? The life of blessed Rosario should be an example for the Catholic lawyers on how we should, as Christians, sanctify our work and our daily lives by serving the common good.

The Life of Blessed Rosario Livatino

Domenico AIROMA
Chief prosecutor of Avellino (Italy)

1. Dignity and Humility

Rosario Angelo Livatino was born in Canicattì, a little town in the very heart of Sicily, on October 3, 1952. He is the only son of Vincenzo Livatino, an employee of the Municipal Tax Office, and of a teacher, Rosalia Corbo.

The life of Blessed Rosario testifies two aspects of the cultural, moral and spiritual education he received.

The first is represented by the strong sense of dignity, due to his awareness of being part of a thousand-year-old tradition of thought. *Centu anni* (which means one hundred years): this was the nickname his classmates gave him, to emphasize the wisdom almost singular for his young age. The second is given by the humility, the authentic one. The humility of who knows that the search for the truth asks for a never-ending effort. The same humility that leads him, when he decides to approach the sacrament of confirmation, to attend a preparation course, sitting in the oratory with the other young people, while he was already thirty.

Dignity and humility will be his moral stars even as a magistrate; first as public prosecutor and then as judge at the Criminal Court of Agrigento.

Dignity in the exercise of a profession that required firmness, especially in a society where it was normal for a judge to be sensitive to pressure and intimidation; where to be independent and to appear as independent was something heroic.

Dignity but also humility; humility in dealing with the citizens he was called to judge.

Rosario felt himself linked to the accused persons by common humanity principles. Never he felt himself as superior. He respected the liberty of the convicted person so much that he did not hesitate, for instance, to go personally to prison in Agrigento in mid-August to release a person in pre-trial detention.

It is also said that, in the presence of the corpse of a murdered chief of the mafia, after a police officer commented positively on the killing, he said: "Before death, those who believe pray, those who do not believe are silent".

2. Under the Protection of God

Rosario was appointed as a judge at the age of 26, on July 18, 1978. "I took the oath [he noted in his diary] from today therefore I am in the judiciary. May God bless me and help me to respect the oath and to behave according to the principles my parents have taught me".

Words were written in red ink: a clear sign of a mission that he felt like the center of his own life. Was the use of the red pen a mere coincidence? It is to be excluded. Rosario carefully kept his diaries and meditated on his writings with great attention and depth. He was never superficial.

Nor can he be said to suffer graphomania. There are only two writings of a certain consistency that he left us: one dedicated to the role of the judge in a changing society and another to the relationship between faith and law. For the rest, we only have his diaries and his judicial decisions. No interviews and no press conference exist.

The use of red ink cannot be, therefore, anecdotal or a mere coincidence; this cannot be the case for a person who was used to think of himself as living "*sub tutela Domini*", under the protection of the Lord.

It's the sign of the beginning of a mission that Rosario felt as his vocation. It is the path assigned to him by God which he was called to carry out. Even in a context where the *Cosa Nostra* frequently knocked-on his parents' door to the extent the local mafia chief of Canicattì lived on the upper floor of the building where the Livatino family lived.

A mission to never betray, even though he realized the danger to his life was imminent.

We know, in fact, from his diaries that he was tormented by the fear of causing a displeasure to his dearest parents. Nevertheless, he did not hesitate to deal with the most dangerous cases; despite the danger, he never wanted a bodyguard to avoid exposing other people to danger.

His colleagues considered him a point of reference, always at his place, from early in the morning till late in the evening. Just a glass of milk for lunch.

It must be also highlighted that when Rosario dealt with *Cosa Nostra*, lots of the most important investigative tools were not yet introduced.

He was left alone against his enemies and martyrdom was not long in coming.

3. Martyrdom – September 21, 1990

The sky was clear, the sun was already warm when Rosario takes off his jacket and gets in his car, his Ford Fiesta. He takes the usual road in direction of the Court of Agrigento.

What were his thoughts then? Going through his diary, we note that in those days Rosario no longer writes. We do not know the reasons for such a sudden silence. We only know that in those days the dangers for his life had grown.

Many signs of a track against him by the mafia started to emerge: especially since he dealt with the proceedings aimed at seizing the assets of *Cosa Nostra*. The mafia could not stand any more that Christian judge, the *santocchio*, as they called him in a negative way.

They hated him both as judge and as a Christian so much that they wanted to kill him, in the initial project, before the Church where Rosario went every morning before work.

Once again, Rosario Livatino was called to make a choice.

Take a long period of vacation or ask for a transfer to another office, perhaps leaving his Sicily, the landscape that represented his life, his flesh. In short, stay in the place God assigned to him, or choose an exile, more comfortable, quieter.

Once again, he did not back down.

The Lord had called him to that mission; the Lord would have assisted him; the Lord would have given him the strength not to give up, not to surrender to those who wanted to be no justice for Sicily.

We like to think that that morning Rosario, carrying those thoughts in his heart, left home, greeted his parents, and went to work.

Like every morning, like every day.

The assassins who have confessed the abomination committed, tell of a man, mortally wounded, who, looking them in the eye, asks: "What have I done to you, picciotti?"

A man is also judged by how he dies, not only just how he lived. His last words were not of hate. He did not appeal to his authority, to his role. His last gesture was a question.

How is it possible that a man, who feels death at hand; who, therefore, has nothing more to ask of earthly life, concern himself almost worrying if he has done a wrong thing, a wrong action that provokes a mortal hate?

It is possible only if we realize who Rosario was; a man who made justice his mission, until the end. "Until" means all his life long.

In asking that question, he reveals himself once again as a righteous man, righteous also in putting his murderers before their consciences.

4. Why the Beatification?

After being given all the facts on his death from Rosario's mother, Saint John Paul II was so impressed that he pronounced that memorable invective against the Mafia, in the Valley of the Temples of Agrigento, recalling that the judgment of God would also come for them.

The process of beatification began precisely due to the willing of Saint John Paul II who called Rosario a martyr of justice and indirectly of the faith. After a lengthy investigation, during which many of his colleagues and even one of his murderers were interviewed, he was beatified on May 9, 2021. In the process, a miracle was also ascertained: a young woman healed from cancer after she had prayed Rosario.

Why the beatification? Why Rosario and not, for instance, Giovanni Falcone or Paolo Borsellino? Rosario was killed in *odium fidei*, as in him the mobsters saw the right judge because a Christian judge. That's the reason.

He is a martyr of faith, of that faith that led him to understand that charity is the reversal of justice.

A model, ultimately, not only for the judiciary and for lawyers, but also for every man engaged in any institutions, for every Christian who intends to serve these loyally without betraying his conscience. Like all the saints, his example has often been misunderstood, sometimes treated almost with mockery, as when he was called "*il giudice ragazzino*", "the little judge"; still today not welcomed as a model by all magistrates. Even so, he is the way out of the moral crisis that the Italian judiciary is going through.

The battle of Rosario, which was a battle of body and soul, was, ultimately, how to combine faith and life, make life consistent with faith, make faith evident in life.

He had a strong and intense Christian spiritual life. His diaries tell of a soul always looking for the light, that light that satisfies the thirst for infinity.

His life both as a judge and as a Christian can be summarized in the following words we can read in his conference about faith and law: to judge means to decide. "To decide is to choose and [...] to choose is one of the most difficult things that man is called to do. To choose light is necessary and no man is absolute light".

Thank you, Blessed Rosario! Thank you also because you have showed that you can go to heaven even being a judge!

The Legal Thinking of Rosario Livatino

by Filippo VARI
Full professor of constitutional law
Università Europea di Roma,
Vice President of the Centro Studi Rosario Livatino[1]

I was asked to take the floor to talk about the legal thinking of Rosario Livatino. The blessed Judge didn't write much. There are two conferences, only available in Italian: the first is about *The Role of the Judge in a Changing Society* (1984) and the second is about *Faith and Law* (1986).[2] I think it would be worth to translate these speeches in English. The two conferences give us interesting suggestions about Livatino's thinking. I will make three points: the importance of natural law; the task of catholic ju-

---

[1] The website of the Centro Studi Rosario Livatino: https://www.centrostudilivatino.it (23.08.2022).

[2] They can be read at the following links: http://www.sol fano.it/canicatti/Ruolo_Giudice.html; http://www.solfan o.it/canicatti/fedeediritto.htm (23.08.2022).

rists; Livatino's vision of the role of the judge in the contemporary society.

1. Natural Law and Positive Law

The first point is about the existence and the importance of natural law. Rosario Livatino is deeply convinced of the need to consider natural law.

As Pope Francis recalled, in a meeting, referring to the question of euthanasia, Livatino observed:

> If the believer's opposition to this law is based on the conviction that human life […] is a divine gift that it is not lawful for man to suffocate or interrupt, so is the opposition of the non-believer, who is based on the conviction that life is protected by natural law, that no positive right can violate or contradict, since it belongs to the sphere of 'unavailable' goods, that neither individuals nor the community can attack.[3]

The link between natural law and positive law here is very clear,[4] even though the same Livatino admits that "it is increasingly difficult", in the modern, occidental and complex societies, "to know and

---

[3] Rosario Livatino, *Faith and Law*, 1986.

[4] M. Ronco, "Fede e giustizia in Rosario Livatino", in Domenico Airoma (ed.) *Rosario Livatino. Giudice santo*, Camerata Picena, 2016, 127.

have accepted the concepts of right and wrong".[5] There is a block of principles that must be respected by every legislative power.[6] It is interesting that the Catechism of the Catholic Church, in order to explain natural law, recalls Cicero, a jurist who lived before Christ:

> For there is a true law: right reason. It is in conformity with nature, is diffused among all men, and is immutable and eternal; its orders summon to duty; its prohibitions turn away from offense [...] To replace it with a contrary law is a sacrilege; failure to apply even one of its provisions is forbidden; no one can abrogate it entirely.[7]

Centuries later, St. Thomas noted that if the law is unjust, it is not a real law.[8]

This elementary truth is not accepted anymore in Europe, as Benedict XVI pointed out in his speech in front of the German Parliament. I quote this passage of the speech of the German Pope:

---

[5] Rosario Livatino, *The Role of the Judge in a Changing Society*, 1984.

[6] W. Waldstein, https://iusetiustitium.com/the-significan ce-of-roman-law-for-the-development-of-european-law/# more-123 (23.08.2022).

[7] Cicero, Rep. III, 22, 33.

[8] M. Ronco, "Fede e giustizia", *op. cit.*, 125.

The idea of natural law is today viewed as a specifically Catholic doctrine, not worth bringing into the discussion in a non-Catholic environment, so that one feels almost ashamed even to mention the term". [Consequently,] there are concerted efforts to recognize only positivism as a common culture and a common basis for law-making, reducing all the other insights and values of our culture to the level of subculture, with the result that Europe vis-à-vis other world cultures is left in a state of culture-lessness and at the same time extremist and radical movements emerge to fill the vacuum.[9]

In this situation, it is more and more important to affirm – as Livatino does – the existence of natural law and to protest and challenge the laws that do not respect it. I quote his words: "Render unto Caesar the things that are Caesar's, means that also Caesar has a natural law he has to respect".[10] In other words, the State must respect "those needs of individuals, of groups, of the community that are indicated by their very human life".[11]

To make an example, Livatino says that the law cannot allow a person to kill another person, since

---

[9] https://www.vatican.va/content/benedict-xvi/en/speeches/2011/september/documents/hf_ben-xvi_spe_20110922_reichstag-berlin.pdf (23.08.2022).

[10] See Rosario Livatino, *Faith and Law, op. cit.*

[11] *Ibid.*

the right to life – that he considers "the most important one [...] for the legal order"[12] – is an inviolable right of the person and so it is not available even from its holder. We may apply this principle to the questions of abortion and euthanasia, as Livatino did.[13]

Summing up this first point about Livatino's legal thinking, we could say: although Livatino is aware that natural law is not a popular subject, he thinks that there is a natural law and that positive law must respect it.

2. The Task of Catholic Jurists

The second issue that I would like to tackle is about the task and the behavior of Catholic Jurists. In other words: what does Livatino's life and his message tell us about being a jurist, while being catholic.

Livatino quotes a speech of Saint John Paul II of 1982 to the Italian Catholic Jurist's Association. The Great Pope spoke about the importance of implementing "Christian ethics in legal science, in legislative, judicial, administrative activity, in all public life".

We can see a practical application of the first speech of the Polish Pope, in which he invited all the

---

12 *Ibid.*

13 See *ibid.*

people: "do not be afraid" and "open wide the doors for Christ", "to his saving power open the boundaries of States, economic and political systems, the vast fields of culture, civilization and development".[14]

In Livatino's life and thinking we see that, as Pope Benedict XVI pointed out, "the Christian message" is "not only «informative» but «performative»". This means, as the Pope said, that "the Gospel is not merely a communication of things that can be known – it is one that makes things happen and is life-changing". The German Pope highlights that "the dark door of time, of the future, has been thrown open" and that "the one who has hope lives differently; the one who hopes has been granted the gift of a new life".[15] In many speeches has Pope Francis recalled this teaching.[16]

---

[14] John Paul II, *Homily of His Holiness John Paul II For the Inauguration of His Pontificate, 22 October 1978*, available on the website of the Vatican: https://www.vatican.va/con tent/john-paul-ii/en/homilies/1978/documents/hf_jp-ii _hom_19781022_inizio-pontificato.html (23.08.2022).

[15] *Spe salvi*, § 2.

[16] *Message of His Holiness Pope Francis for The 54th World Communications Day*, available on the website of the Vatican: https://www.vatican.va/content/francesco/en/mess ages/communications/documents/papa-francesco_20200 124_messaggio-comunicazioni-sociali.html (23.08.2022).

In one of his two conferences, Livatino states that there is not indifference between the political society and the faith: "there is not absolute separation but a correct relationship" between them.[17] In other words, religion is not only a private matter, but has a concrete influence in public life.

Livatino was beatified by the Catholic Church. He had a normal life. He didn't do any wonder during his life. When he was killed by the mafia, as Pope Francis noted,

> almost no one knew him, [since] he worked in a suburban court: he dealt with the seizure and confiscation of property of illegal origin acquired by the mafia. [However, the Pope says,] he did so in an unassailable manner, respecting the guarantees of the accused, with great professionalism and with concrete results: for this reason the mafia decided to eliminate him.[18]

---

[17] Rosario Livatino, *Faith and Law, op. cit.*; see M. Ronco, "Fede e giustizia", *op. cit.*, 126.

[18] Pope Francis, *Address of His Holiness Pope Francis to Members of the „Rosario Livatino" Study Center,* November 29, 2019, in the Website of the Vatican: https://www.vatican.va/content/francesco/en/speeches/2019/november/documents/papa-francesco_20191129_centrostudi-rosariolivatino.html (23.08.2022).

Operari sequitur esse (what we do always expresses what we are), as saint Thomas thought.[19]

In performing his daily duties, Livatino found the path to sanctity. He did his job without sensationalism, aware of the difficulties of the task to judge other men.

As Mauro Ronco pointed out, Livatino felt the great responsibility of his job, not only on the civil ground, but moreover on the moral one, and he found it necessary for the believer to look at God and for the non-believer to look at the conscience inspired by the common good.[20]

Livatino said:

To decide is to choose [...]; and to choose is one of the most difficult things that man is called to do. And it is precisely in this choice to decide, to decide to order, that the believing magistrate can find a relationship with God. A direct relationship, because doing justice is self-realization, it is prayer, it is self-dedication to God. An indirect relationship, through love for the person judged.

Livatino goes on:

The non-believing magistrate replaces reference to the transcendent with reference to the social body,

---

[19] Regarding the application of this principle to Livatino's life see M. Ronco, "Fede e giustizia", *op. cit.*, 122.

[20] *Ibid.*, 134.

in a different sense but with equal spiritual commitment. [...] And such a task will be all the lighter the more the magistrate will humbly be aware of his own weaknesses, the more he will present himself each time to society willing and inclined to understand the man in front of him and to judge him without the attitude of a superman, but rather with constructive contrition.[21]

Livatino is very aware of Jesus' teaching and refers to it: "Let the one among you who is without sin be the first to throw a stone at her".[22] The Blessed Judge says about his job: "sin is shadow and you need light to judge, but no man is absolute light".

If we had to sum up this second point of Livatino's mandate, I would say that a catholic jurist is a person who not only believes in Jesus, but tries to make his teaching performing his daily activities and, amongst them, his job.

3. The Role of the Judge and the Society

We come so at my third point. It concerns Livatino's teaching on the role of the judge in the contemporary society. At the time when Livatino lived, there was already a debate that goes on nowadays on the role of the judge and about how much he can bend

---

[21] Rosario Livatino, *Faith and Law, op. cit.*

[22] John 8:7.

the wording of the law in order to achieve a better decision. Being himself a judge, Livatino reflects about which type of attitude judges should have.

In this conference, that is also related to money laundering, it is interesting to reflect on the picture of the judge Livatino draws. I quote a long passage of his conference:

> The judge's independence is not only in his conscience, in his moral freedom, in his loyalty to principles, in his capacity for sacrifice, in his technical knowledge, in his experience, in the clarity and linearity of his decisions; but also in his morality, in the transparency of his conduct even outside the walls of his office, in the normality of his relations and manifestations in social life, in the choice of his friendships, in his unwillingness to take up initiatives and business ventures, albeit permissible but risky, in his renunciation of any desire for appointments and easy profits, especially in sectors that, by their nature or the implications they entail, can produce the seed of contamination and the danger of interference; the judge's independence lies finally in his credibility, which he succeeds in gaining in the travails of his decisions and at every moment of his activity.[23]

---

[23] Rosario Livatino, *The Role of the Judge in a Changing Society*, *op. cit.*

We see here how high the standards are Livatino expects from judges. They go a lot further than what they are obliged to by law. In his eyes judges should also be very cautious in their private lives in order to be truly independent and in order also to appear so. Of course, this is also influenced by the difficult situation of Sicily, where the mafia, for instance, tends to be present in areas of the economic life of the Island. Let me adapt the famous phrase: Justice must not only be done, it must also seen to be done. I think Livatino would fully agree with the following sentence: judges not only should be independent, they should also be seen to be independent. At the end of the day, one could pick out one word for this whole bunch of external and internal attitudes Livatino refers to: personal credibility.

Livatino examines the role of the judge in his relationship with the society also from the point of view of the increasing pressure on him – taking place in Italy from the '60 onwards as I said before – "to fix a new relationship between his role and the evolution of society, exalting the power of interpretation of the law" and giving the judge a political role.[24] Respecting Montesquieu's teaching, Livatino clearly states that the judge must observe

---

[24] *Ibid.*

his constitutional duty of loyalty to the law, [since he] is nothing more than an employee of the State to whom is entrusted the very special task of applying the laws that society gives itself through its institutions".[25]

Livatino refuses the idea that the judge can substitute himself to the legislative power, looking for the right solution of the case, to apply at the place of the one stated by the law.[26] To use the words of the very well-know decision Marbury v. Madison of the US Supreme Court,[27] "it is emphatically the province and duty of the judiciary to say what the law is", not to decide on a political judgement what it could be.[28]

Livatino says that "the judge must bend its own convictions to the law and not the law to its convictions".[29]

As Pope Francis pointed out,

---

[25] *Ibid.*

[26] *Ibid.*, Canicattì, 7 April 1984.

[27] https://www.archives.gov/milestone-documents/marbury-v-madison#:~:text=It%20is%20emphatically%20the%20province,on%20the%20operation%20of%20each (23.08.2022).

[28] See The Federalist Society website, at the address https://fedsoc.org/about-us.

[29] Rosario Livatino, *The Role of the Judge in a Changing Society*, *op. cit.*

also in this regard, the relevance of Rosario Livatino is surprising, because he grasps the signs of what would have emerged most clearly in the following decades, not only in Italy, that is, the justification of the encroachment of the judge in areas not proper to the role, especially in the areas of so-called «new rights», with judgments that seem to be concerned with fulfilling ever new desires, unencumbered by any objective limit.[30]

We could summarize this third point of Livatino's legal thinking about the relationship between the judge and the society: on one hand, the judge is like Caesar's wife, who "must be above suspicions"; and on the other hand, the judge must respect its function to apply the laws approved by the People through its representatives, the Parliament, and refuse a political role through judicial activism.

Conclusion

The considerations above show the profound vitality of Livatino's legal thinking.

His example constitutes a point of reference for all of us who are Catholic jurists. As the Chief Prosecutor of Rome, Dr. Lo Voi, said, Livatino should be "like Hippocrates for medical doctors, [...] a

---

[30] Pope Francis, *Address of His Holiness Pope Francis to Members of the „Rosario Livatino" Study Center, op. cit.*

point of reference for every magistrate" or, I would add, as Domenico Airoma said, for all the "jurists, but also for every man engaged in institutions, for every Christian who intends to serve these loyally without betraying his conscience".

May Blessed Livatino help us from heaven to make our contribution to society, committing ourselves as jurists to respect and promote natural law in the contemporary legal orders in which we work.

The Purpose of AML Law Rules and Inspirational AML Lawyers

Claude EISCHEN
European delegated prosecutor[1]

The purpose of this last contribution is to underline the absolute necessity of fighting money laundering and the financing of terrorism. Then to identify, if any, contemporary "inspirational AML lawyers".

1. The Purpose of AML Law Rules

As a starting point, it is good to define what anti-money laundering (AML) means. Article 3 of the UN Vienna 1988 Convention states that AML means

> the conversion or transfer of property, knowing that such property is derived from any offense(s),

[1] Please note that Claude Eischen's intervention was given in a private capacity and not as *European delegated prosecutor*. This edited transcript does not reflect the views of the *European Public Prosecutor's Office* as an institution.

for the purpose of concealing or disguising the illicit origin of the property or of assisting any person who is involved in such offense(s) to evade the legal consequences of his actions.

In practical terms, this means that if you have dirty money, you cannot use it as such to the extent you will be questioned on the origins of the funds you are trying to inject in the economy. The integration of dirty money into the financial system is a three-step operation: placement, layering and integration. This mechanism is illustrated in the below slide 1.

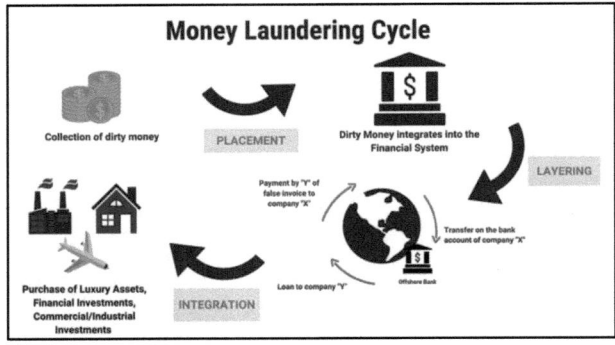

Slide 1: Money Laundering Cycle
(source: European Public Prosecutor's Office)

The strategies following which you can perform money laundering are diverse. The slide 2 illustrates the various methods of money laundering such as false invoicing, informal methods of transferring money (the so-called *Hawala*) or flying money (*Fei-Chein*), and the integration of criminal funds.

Slide 2: **Money Laundering Features**[2]

Trade Based Money Laundering – False invoicing and over-invoicing
- Companies without any real economic existence used as invoices-makers
- High-value goods as electronics and luxury cars / Services as consulting, marketing or fees
- Gates to channel to or retrieve funds from non-cooperating jurisdictions
- Companies and transactions chains provided by Professional Money Launderers

Money or Value Transfer Systems – Hawala and Fei-Chien
- As a service provided to OCGs related with PIF crimes
- Illicit funds from VAT fraud are made available to criminals in cash via hawalers/fei-chien
- Cash is partially re-deposited on missing traders bank accounts to reinitiate a predicate crime (VAT fraud especially) or to continue the money laundering circuit

Real Estate and touristic activities investment – Integration of criminal funds
- EU funds as an investment possibility by OCGs
- Funds derived from other criminal activities are integrated (as self-investment) on projects co-financed by EU

---

[2] Source: European Public Prosecutor's Office.

- Once the projects concluded, the properties or assets are sold/transferred generating considerable profits

The amount of dirty moneys circulating in the global economy is estimated by the United Nations between 800 and 2 000 billion dollars. To illustrate such amounts, 2 000 billion dollars is the estimated GDP for Italy in 2022. We are talking about massive figures which represent a material threat to the functioning of market economies and states. In this respect, GAFI (or FATF) has declared recently that the amount of dirty money which is injected in the economy via money laundering mechanisms is so massive that it allows organised crime to take control over entire sectors of the economy and enables them to corrupt administrations and even entire governments. Thus money laundering can be identified as creating intense societal risks.

Historically, the first attempt to fight money laundering was made in North America during the Prohibition. Then, the second wave was implemented with the fight against international drug trafficking. And the last step was the fight against the financing of terrorism after 9/11.

As a result, fighting against money laundering and terrorism is accepted by a majority of citizens as a "legitimate" public policy and in the interest of all to the extent its aims to preserve political and economic stability within democracies and states. If identifying the negative impact of dirty money is a straightforward matter, the means to combat it is far more complex issue.

An ever-increasing number of laws and regulations have been implemented in the last decades. They are in constant evolution for the simple reason that the money launderers can circumvent the latest norms by finding creative ways to by-pass the latest AML rules. Therefore, the legislator is in a constant need to legislate.

Big firms are coping with these AML regulatory obligations and are able to hire "regiments" of low- and mid- level compliance officers. Big firms have launched specific recruitment campaigns to hire these so-called "AML heroes" (see the slide 3) to cope with the numerous challenges brought by the robust EU and national AML legislation. In contrast, small companies are struggling to follow and to implement these norms. The situation is sometimes difficult for some market players (which struggle to conform with the AML requirements due to lack of resources) In one instance, the tax regulator decided to do some name shaming to oblige more than forty real estate companies to comply with the Luxembourg AML rules (see the slide 4).

Claude Eischen

Slide 3: ABN AMRO[3]

Slide 4: Paperjam[4]

---

[3] See https://www.abnamro.com/en/news/abn-amro-presents-movie-in-search-of-hundreds-of-anti-money-laundering (27.07.2022).

[4] https://paperjam.lu/article/inedit-name-and-shame-contre-s#: ~:text=Le%20directeur%20de%20l%27Administration,aux%20

The latest figures available for Luxembourg also illustrate the impact of the *Cellule de Renseignement Financier* (CRF). Out of the 197 AML reports submitted by the CRF to the Luxembourg jurisdictions, 108 are related to fraud, 45 to money laundering, 5 to criminal tax infractions, 3 to corruption, and 3 to terrorism or financing of terrorism (CRF annual report of 2020, dated December 2021).

2. Identifying "Inspirational AML Lawyers"

After doing some research and trying to identify a list of "inspirational lawyers" having been involved in the fight against money laundering, the results are slightly disappointing. Indeed, inspirational AML lawyers having illustrated themselves recently in the fight against AML perpetrators are surprisingly not numerous.

We can name of course Rosario Livatino and closer to us, the acting European Chief Prosecutor, namely Laura Codruta Kövesi. Ms Kovesi is an outstanding figure in this respect. Prior joining the EU prosecution office, she was in charge of the Romanian National Anticorruption Directorate. During her time at the helm of this institution, she has realised an outstanding job by successfully incriminating and

nouvelles%20r%C3%A8gles%20anti%2Dblanchiment (27.07.2022).

pursuing 14 active and former ministers, 30 members of the Romanian parliament, 4 Romanian senators, 1 MEP, 8 State counsellors, and 31 presidents of county councils! This has enabled the Romanian state to seize assets of around 2 billion euros! Her legacy is without comment. When recently visiting the Italian Republic as the European Chief Prosecutor, Ms Kövesi has stated that her action was in the continuity of the outstanding legacy of Italian judges such as judge Falcone or judge Borsellino who have paid with their lives when fighting the mafia.

When identifying recent judges having been involved in important AML cases, the name of the Brazilian judge Sergio Moro can be raised in the Petrobras Scandal of 2014 was extensively covered by the media, books and even Netflix series. However, all the elements of this case are not entirely clear, and the political dimension does not help to shed light on the whole scandal.

A more recent case (dated 2018) is the 1 Malaysia Development Berhad scandal which involved wrongdoings and personal enrichment by the former Prime Minister of Malaysia. This whole case was initiated by a whistle blower who provided relevant material to a journalist who in turn brought public attention to this affair. No lawyers were involved at the outset of this case.

The most recent affair is the murder of the anti-narcotic Paraguayan persecutor Marcelo Pecci. He was killed by the mafia in May 2022 during his honeymoon in Columbia. The rare courage of Pecci in fighting the local mafia needs to be underlined.

Conclusion

As a summary, we have not identified many "AML inspirational lawyers" besides the outstanding figures of several judges and prosecutors who have paid with their lives to fight the mafia. We have noted that whistle-blowers and journalists have in turn played recently an important role in this struggle. Needless to say that fighting against dirty money and its laundering is a matter of concern for any citizen and especially us, lawyers.

Conclusion

by Olivier DE PINIEUX
Compliance manager and Treasurer of the Catholic
Law Society of Luxembourg

The fight against money laundering and the financing of terrorism is and should be a priority for our democratic societies.

Rosario Livatino is a key person and an example in the war against dirty money. He should be a model for compliance officers, judges and prosecutors, and any AML practitioner.

Since the 90s, a "tsunami" of AML laws and regulations has been implemented to fight dirty money with an increasing efficiency. However, the recent death of prosecutor Pecci shows that this is an ongoing struggle for any righteous women or men of law and beyond. Livatino's last words were: "what have I done to you, picciotti?".

All about the *Conférence Saint-Yves*, the Luxembourg Catholic Law Society

by William Lindsay SIMPSON
President of the Catholic Law Society
of Luxembourg

The oldest Law Society in Luxembourg. The *Conférence Saint-Yves* (CSY) was founded in 1916.

At the service of the legal community. The CSY organises conferences and events on a monthly basis with the aim of contributing to the EU and Luxembourg legal and judicial life. The CSY always tries to address legal matters pedagogically, in a non-profitable way and by instilling dynamic or prospective thinking on any relevant legal or regulatory matter. It aims to clarify complex legal issues and to bring all the various members of the Luxembourg legal community around the same table[1].

---

[1] For more information, see: Mark Jeck, "Von Cannabis, Reliquien und Mafiajägern", *Luxemburger Wort* (Luxembourg), October 15, 2021, p. 24; William Lindsay Simp-

The legal materials related to the events of the CSY are all available on its website www.csy.lu.

Catholic DNA. Beside its mission at the service of the legal community, the CSY is well-aware of its Catholic DNA. In addition to celebrating an annual mass at the beginning of the judicial year (every Autumn), its annual "Banquet of the Saint-Yves" is organized during the month of June and includes a mass in the honour of its patron saint and a speech by a high-profile legal personality (including recently the presidents of the CJEU, the ECHR…). The CSY has further initiated a reflection on Canon law, on Catholic identity, faith and culture, and even beyond this by being interested in Christianity in a more general sense. In this respect, the CSY has published in October 2022 a book which includes all the conferences it has organized on the Christian Presence in the Holy Land (Orthodox, Protestants, Copts…)[2].

---

son, "Continuité et renaissance de l'association des avocats et des juristes catholiques au Luxembourg", *ALUC Contact* 2021-2 (Luxembourg), pp. 22-25; Nicolas Duchesne, Lionel Grzegorczyk, William Lindsay Simpson, "Le rôle de la Conférence Saint-Yves dans la vie juridique luxembourgeoise", *Legimag* No. 20 (Luxembourg), December 2017, pp. 29-30.

[2] William Lindsay Simpson (ed.), "Laudate Jerusalem, La présence chrétienne en Terre sainte", *Parole et Silence*, 2022, pp. 1-179.